# WHISPERS OF MANDALA

Get lost with the charming patterns

# This book belongs to :

________________________

By: Danelle Plattlov

Livreopolis

# Thank you for your purchase !

We sincerely hope you enjoyed this book.
Please let us know if we can do anything to help!

Your feedback and suggestions can do miracles for us.
Please do not hesitate to let us know how you like the book at:

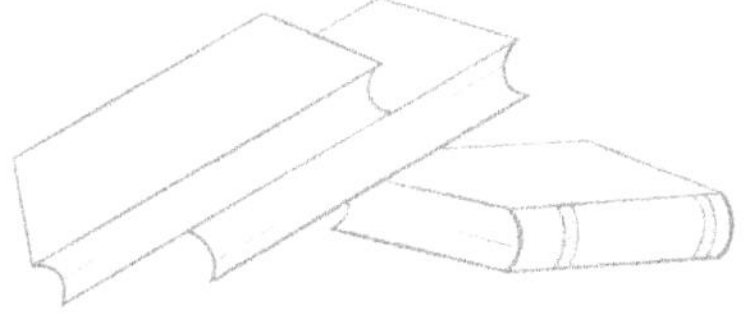

www.ingramcontent.com/pod-product-compliance
Lightning Source LLC
Chambersburg PA
CBHW080030260726
48658CB00007B/2548

# Thank you for your purchase !

We sincerely hope you enjoyed this book.
Please let us know if we can do anything to help!

Your feedback and suggestions can do miracles for us.
Please do not hesitate to let us know how you like the book at:

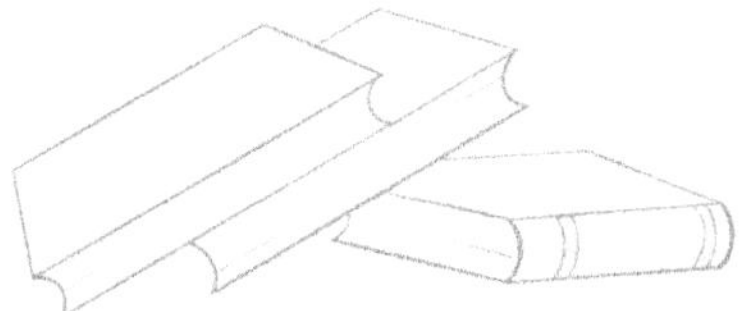